T0379607

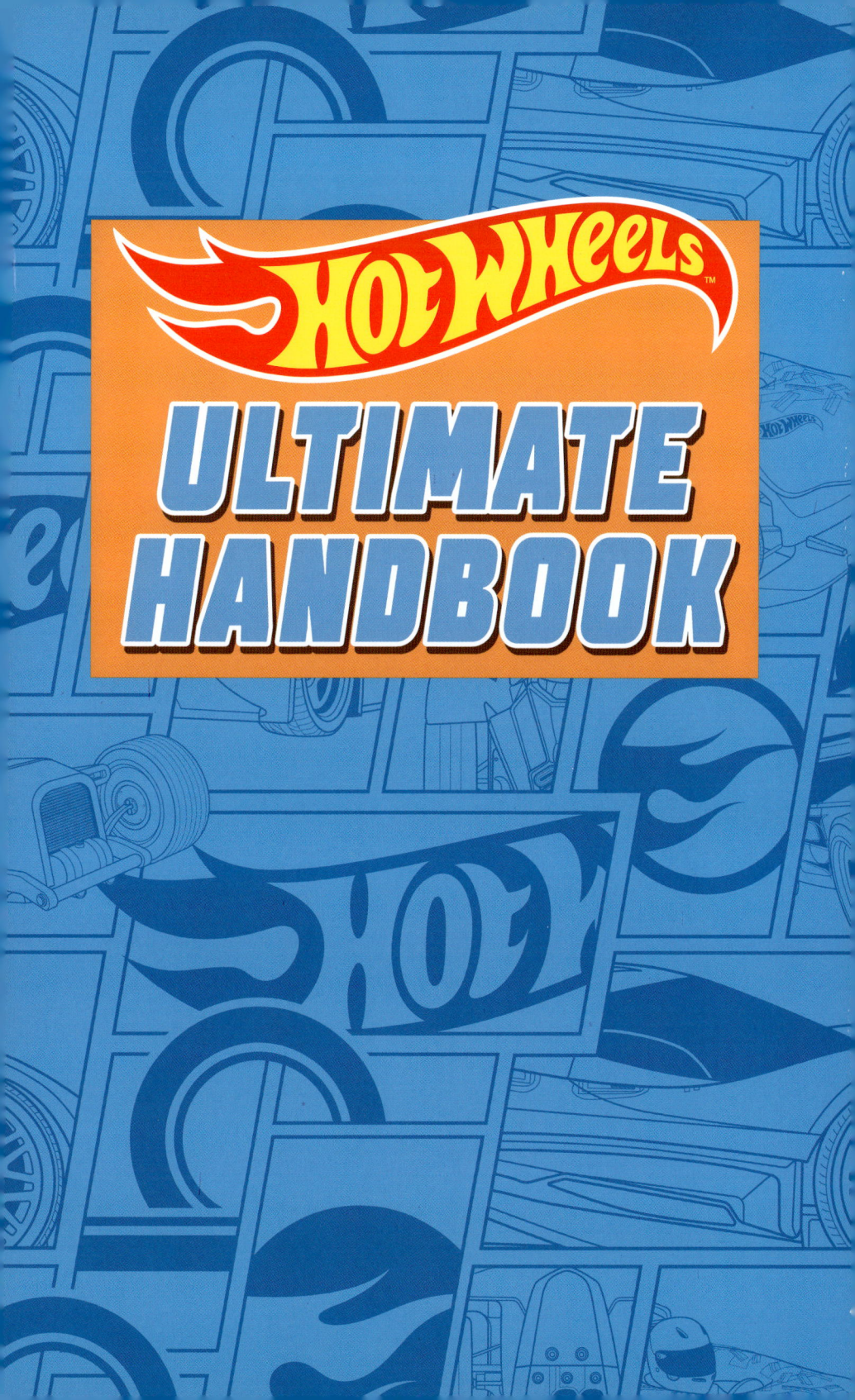

ACKNOWLEDGMENTS

Many thanks to the Mattel Press team, including Ryan Ferguson, Samantha Schutz, Elaine Gant, Jenny Yee, Karen Painter, Kate Milford, Rowenna Otazu, Kirstie Watkins, and Alix Rosenberg.

And thanks to the many other Mattel employees who kept us on the right track, including Roberto Stanichi, Andrea Vitali, Ryan Lusk, Melissa Telle, Megan Kunc, Jimmy Liu, Craig Callum, Katherine Eng, Dwayne Vance, Andrew Lubetsky, Matt Gabe, Audrey Seto, Jennifer Kobashi, Melissa Huntington, Eliana Ruiz, Sheila Tan-Chan, Donyelle Evans, Will Hird, Lexi Ronnestrand, Jacob Wells, and Gonzalo Estrada Ortiz.

We are also grateful to these Mattel photographers for their contributions: David Chickering, Teri Weber, Jeff O'Brien, Colby Liebelt, and Larry Bartholomew.

All images are property of Mattel unless otherwise noted.
Page 28: (top) © NBC; (bottom) © James Stack/NBC

ISBN 9781683432197
11 10 9 8 7 6 5 4 3 2
This edition first printing, January 2025
Printed in China QP
Written by Orli Zuravicky
Designed by Mark Golden
Visit us at Mattel.com.

HOT WHEELS™

ULTIMATE HANDBOOK

A GUIDE TO 160+ ORIGINAL DESIGNS

MATTEL Press™

TABLE OF CONTENTS

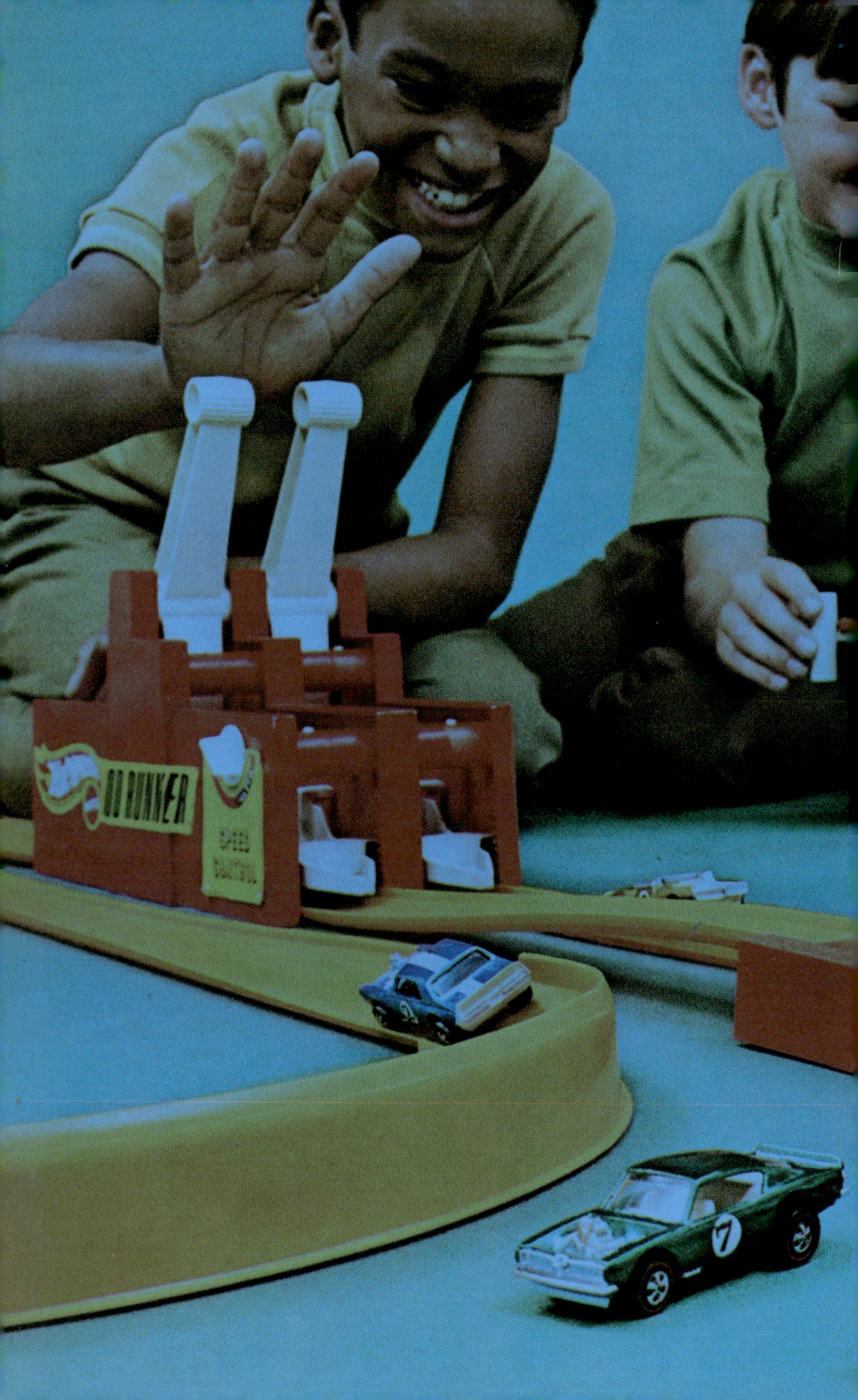

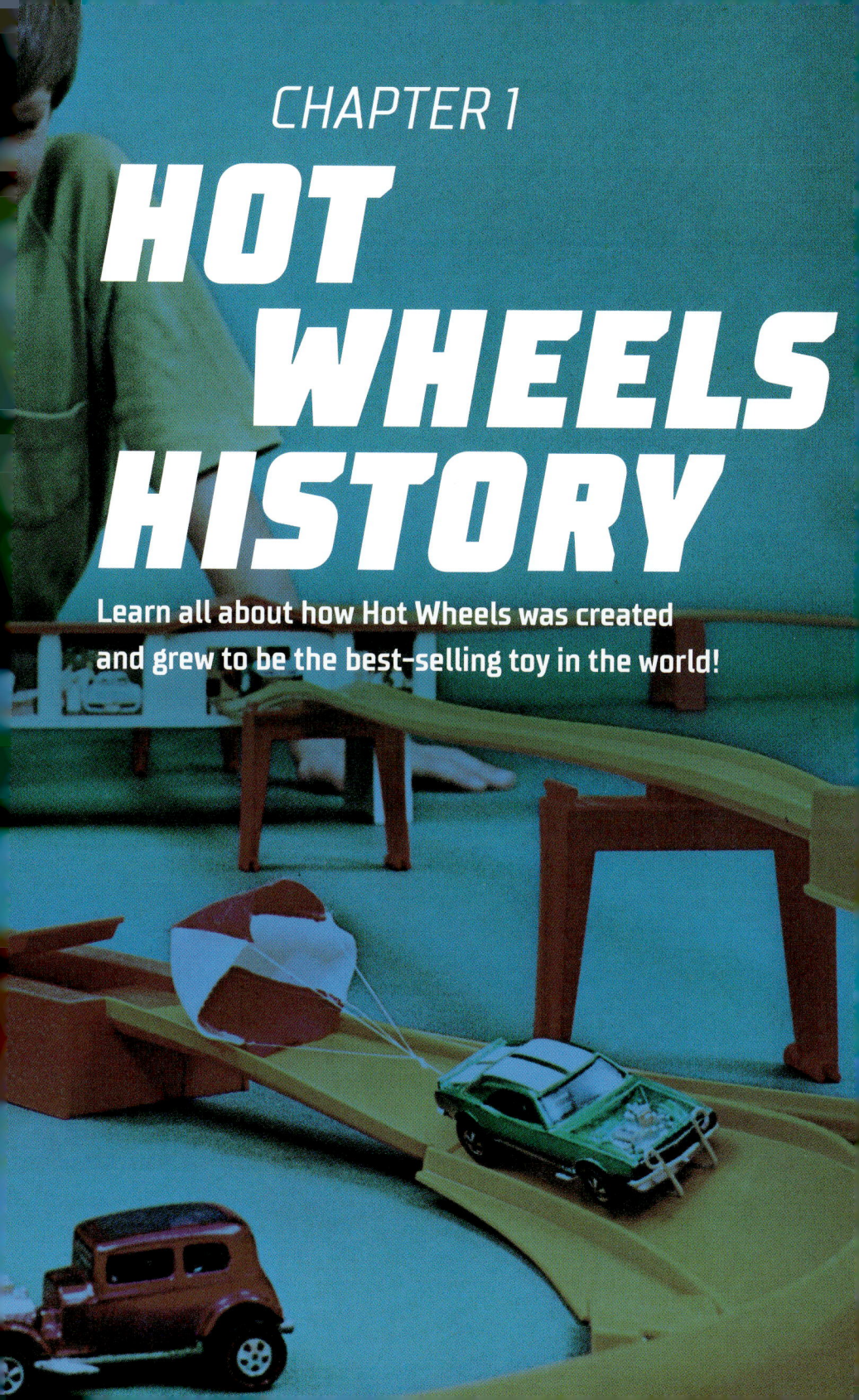

CHAPTER 1

HOT WHEELS HISTORY

Learn all about how Hot Wheels was created and grew to be the best-selling toy in the world!

HOT WHEELS THEN

Like all great things, Hot Wheels started as an idea. The 1960s was an exciting time in California, especially in the world of hot rods—cars that were rebuilt or modified for speed. Elliot Handler, co-founder of Mattel, and Ruth Handler, president of Mattel and Elliot's wife, had young grandchildren who loved to play with die-cast cars made by Mattel's competitors. Elliot studied those cars and noticed they couldn't go that far or that fast. He knew he could make a better car—a new kind of car that captured the spirit and thrill of the California car culture.

Elliot thought that the problem with the competitive cars was that they were created mostly to collect and admire. Mattel's new cars would have real wheels that could truly spin and build speed.

In 1966, Elliot and a few people on his team built and tested a prototype. Handler was so impressed by the car's groundbreaking, new wheel design and performance that his first response when he saw it rolling along the floor was: "Those are some hot wheels!" And so, the Hot Wheels brand was born. The first sixteen cars launched in 1968.

Hot Wheels produces 130 new car designs annually and there are more than 25,000 different existing variations. About two thirds of the line are cars made in partnership with the world's most famous car companies. The other one-third are Hot Wheels Originals, new fantasy cars developed by the brand's talented designers. Whether these originals are silly, fantastical, or look like they could have been designed by a real automotive company, they are always rooted in automotive authenticity.

Since the brand's launch, Hot Wheels has become the best-selling toy line in the world. Today, Hot Wheels are sold in 150 different countries. 500 million toy cars are manufactured each year, and it's estimated that sixteen Hot Wheels are sold per second!

HOT WHEELS THROUGH THE YEARS

Choose from 16 new California custom styled Hot Wheels!

1966
A New American Icon
Elliot Handler and his colleagues set out to create a new line of toys that innovate vehicle play and tap into the thrill of the custom hot rod culture.

1968
The Original 16
Hot Wheels launches with sixteen iconic, custom cars. These originals are among the most valuable toys of all time.

1988
Hot Wheels Launches Color Changers
This innovation allows kids to change the colors, stripes, numbers, and decos of their cars by dipping them into water of various temperatures.

1991
The Billion Cars Club
Hot Wheels proudly produces its one-billionth car!

1969
Hot Wheels Originals
The very first Hot Wheels Original, the Twin Mill, debuts. The Twin Mill is considered one of the brand's most iconic cars.

1983
Real Riders Roll In
Hot Wheels debuts die-casts with real rubber tires. These cars are highly collectible since the line didn't last long due to high costs.

2001
Hot Wheels in Real Life
The first ever full-size, drivable Hot Wheels car is created—based on the iconic Twin Mill. Since then, Hot Wheels has brought more than twenty other cars to life.

2006
A New Classic
The Bone Shaker is first released.

HOT WHEELS THROUGH THE YEARS

2011
Indy 500 World Record
Dropping from the top of a 100-foot-tall, life-size version of the iconic orange track, Team Hot Wheels jumps 332 feet, crushing the previous record by an impressive thirty-one feet!

2012
World Record at the X Games
Two Loop Coupes set a Guinness World Record when they defy gravity and complete the Hot Wheels Double Dare Loop stunt.

2018

50th Anniversary

On May 16, Hot Wheels celebrates this milestone with new collectibles and a lineup of live experiences, including the Hot Wheels Legends Tour, the search for a custom vehicle worthy of becoming a Hot Wheels die-cast car.

2021

Hot Wheels Unleashed

Mattel releases *Hot Wheels Unleashed*—an action-packed video game where gamers can get behind the wheel of 130 of the coolest cars and vehicles. *Hot Wheels Unleashed 2* is released in 2024.

2023

Hot Wheels Ultimate Challenge

Mattel launches a reality competition show where contestants give vehicles Hot Wheels-style makeovers. The winner receives $50,000 and has their design turned into a die-cast toy.

2024

Hot Wheels Let's Race

Mattel launches this animated series for kids on Netflix. It is viewed more than four million times in the first week!

CHAPTER 2

UNDER THE HOOD

Find out how Hot Wheels die-cast cars are made, learn about collecting, and take a peek into the jobs of two people on the Hot Wheels team at Mattel.

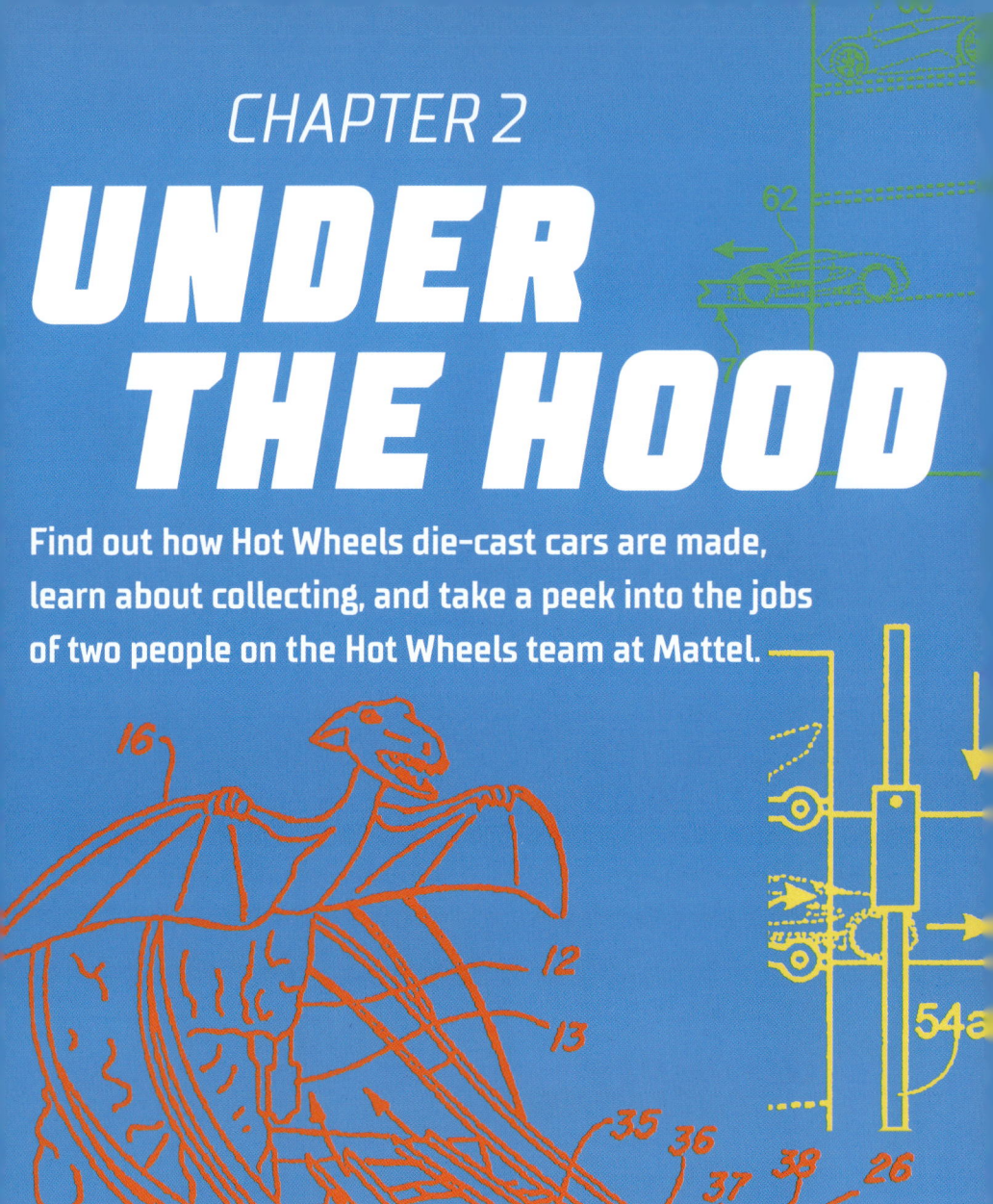

HOW HOT WHEELS ARE MADE

Have you ever wondered how your favorite Hot Wheels car is made? Let's check out how Mattel does it!

1 First, the designer sketches out the car. This can happen with a pencil and paper, or with a software program on the computer.

2 Once the sketch is finalized, it's time to virtual-sculpt it into a three-dimensional version of the car. Designers use computer-aided design software (CAD) with a special digital pen (a stylus) to build a clay-like model of the car. This stage can take forty hours or more!

3 Next, the car is parted (separated) into the chassis (frame), body, windows, interior, and four wheels. The designers make sure the parts' dimensions will work with the existing Hot Wheels toy tracks and that the 1:64 scale model is as accurate and detailed as possible.

4 After the model is complete, the file is sent to a 3D (three-dimensional) printer. The 3D models are about three inches long. As the models are tested, adjustments are made until the designers are happy with the final design.

5 The final design is sent to the factory so that a die (mold) can be created. Then the mold is filled with liquid metal until it hardens. This is called "casting." That's where the word "die-cast" comes from. Any last imperfections are smoothed out by hand, and the cars are ready to be produced by the thousands.

Once the cars are produced, they are packaged and shipped to stores for fans to buy.

YOU CAN COLLECT THEM ALL!

Do you want to be a Hot Wheels collector? Do you already have a collection that you want to grow? Here are some tips and tricks to hunt for your favorite vehicles.

Color:
Have a favorite hue? Try collecting only cars in that color, or maybe just a specific type of vehicle in that color.

Type:
Do you like trucks or sports cars? Coupes or sedans? Whatever type of vehicle you're into, you can start collecting them all.

Value:
Interested in collecting the Hot Wheels cars worth the most money? Here are three factors to keep in mind when considering value: rarity, originality, and condition.

Accessories:
Die-cast vehicles aren't the only Hot Wheels items to collect. There are carrying cases, racetracks, clothes, and even comic books!

WHAT'S ON THE BOX?

Every Hot Wheels toy comes in iconic packaging that—let's face it—is pretty compact! Even so, it's chock full of very useful information, especially for collectors. Here's a short list of what information you should look for on the box and where to find it.

Collector Number
This is the collector number for the year the car is released

Special Feature
This identifies that this vehicle has a special feature—you can read all about it on the back of the packaging.

Mini Collection
First is the collector number for the mini collection. The icon identifies the mini collection. The color bar holds the name of the mini collection and its signature color.

Vehicle Name
This is the official name of the vehicle.

What makes you excited to come to work every day?
My best days at work are when we get our production samples from the factory. Seeing our ideas come to life is so rewarding.

What is the most surprising part of your job?
I never imagined how many interviews, articles, and events I'd be invited to do so I could explain my job. And having fans ask me to sign my designs is always a shock!

What was your dream job when you were a kid?
At the age of five, I wanted to be a car designer!

What's your job on the Hot Wheels team?
I get to draw and make new Hot Wheels cars with my awesome team of designers.

And the most challenging?
We make so many cars every year that sometimes it's hard to keep track of all the schedules. Luckily, I have an incredible team to help me with that!

Can you share a time when a design went wrong?

Being wrong is an important part of design; we never get it right the first time. And that makes the final design so much better! For every car I have designed that gets made into a die-cast, there are probably twenty others that didn't work out.

What's the strangest part of your job?

The Experimotors line is filled with wacky ideas, so working on one of those vehicles is always pretty odd. When I was thinking about what a car would look like if it had a mustache comb stashed in the middle of it, I stepped back and thought, I have a wild job.

What kind of education or courses did you take to be able to do your job?

I studied art, design, math, and physics. I also got a degree in transportation design. I worked in the automotive industry for a few years before finding the toy world, and eventually, the Hot Wheels team.

What tools do you use to do your job?

It all starts with a simple pen and paper. We may use design software such as Photoshop, Procreate, and CAD. These tools help us refine our drawings or make them 3D.

Where do you get your inspiration for new car designs?

As a car enthusiast, I am always looking at cars, reading about new models, and checking out events where people have modified their cars. I also look at current fashion trends and try to predict where they might head since we are designing our cars two years before they go on sale. Inspiration also comes from the talented designers on my team. They are always talking about cars they've seen, sharing ideas, and offering feedback.

MEET
KATHERINE ENG
Hot Wheels Development Manager

What was your dream job when you were a kid?

I had a few different phases where I wanted to be an Olympic swimmer, a marine biologist, and a pediatrician. I was never really set on one thing; I thought I could be anything if I worked hard at it.

What's your job on the Hot Wheels team?

I make sure the toys are being made on time and on budget.

What's the most challenging part of your job?

Having so many projects going at the same time can be challenging. There's only so much time in a day to get things done and when everything feels important, it can be hard to choose what to do first.

What's the most surprising part of your job?

How detailed we get during the toy-making process! Many people think it's just a simple toy car, but so much time and effort go into everything we do.

What makes you excited to come to work every day?

Finally being able to see the product that the team has been planning and developing for months. It's also so fun to share in the excitement with my teammates!

What's the strangest part of your job?

Talking about cars! My automotive knowledge was pretty limited before I started working at Mattel, but now I know some pretty cool car facts.

What is the best part and most challenging part about working with so many different teams?

The best part is being able to interact with so many different people—from the team in California to our colleagues in Asia. When I first started though, working with so many people made it a challenge to remember their roles in the development process.

Can you share a time when a project went wrong and how you got back on track?

Things can go wrong all the time! It's part of the process. I try to be ready for problems and roadblocks, but there will always be surprises. So, when a problem does come up, it's important to communicate with the team so we can work together to find the best solution.

CHAPTER 3

HOT WHEELS NOW

Learn all about how Hot Wheels was created and grew to be the best-selling toy in the world!

WELCOME TO THE

HOT WHEELS GARAGE OF LEGENDS™

Have you ever wished that your favorite Hot Wheels toy cars would come to life? Welcome to the Garage of Legends, an elite collection of life-size Hot Wheels vehicles that represent the most creative, original, and powerful Hot Wheels of all time.

The very first life-size car debuted in 2001. Today, the Garage boasts more than twenty full-scale Hot Wheels vehicles built for speed and ready for the real-life racetrack. What car do you want to join the Garage of Legends?

THE SEARCH FOR THE NEXT LEGEND

Hot Wheels is always on the lookout for custom-built cars worthy of being called a Hot Wheels Legend. So, in 2018, Mattel created the first Hot Wheels Legends Tour, bringing together custom-car-builders from all over the world to show off their real-life creations. One winning car each year gets bragging rights to be called a Legend, and their design gets made into an official Hot Wheels die-cast car.

What makes a Hot Wheels Legend? Great question! Authenticity and creativity are top of the list. Also, a car that shows "garage spirit." That means the creator worked long hours and their build shows grit, determination, and passion.

Ready to see Hot Wheels come to life? *Hot Wheels Ultimate Challenge* is a reality show where contestants give real-life cars Hot Wheels-style makeovers. In each episode, two contestants work with expert mechanics to design and build their Hot Wheels dream car.

In the end, three finalists compete for the $50,000 grand prize and the chance to have their design turned into a die-cast Hot Wheels toy.

A brand-new generation of racers
heads to the Ultimate Garage in *Hot Wheels Let's Race*,
the animated series as seen on Netflix. In this action-packed show,
six kid-racers put the pedal to the metal in mind-blowing races, thrilling
challenges, and extreme stunts. Each car has a special power, and these
kids get to race them all. **Go, Hot Wheels!**

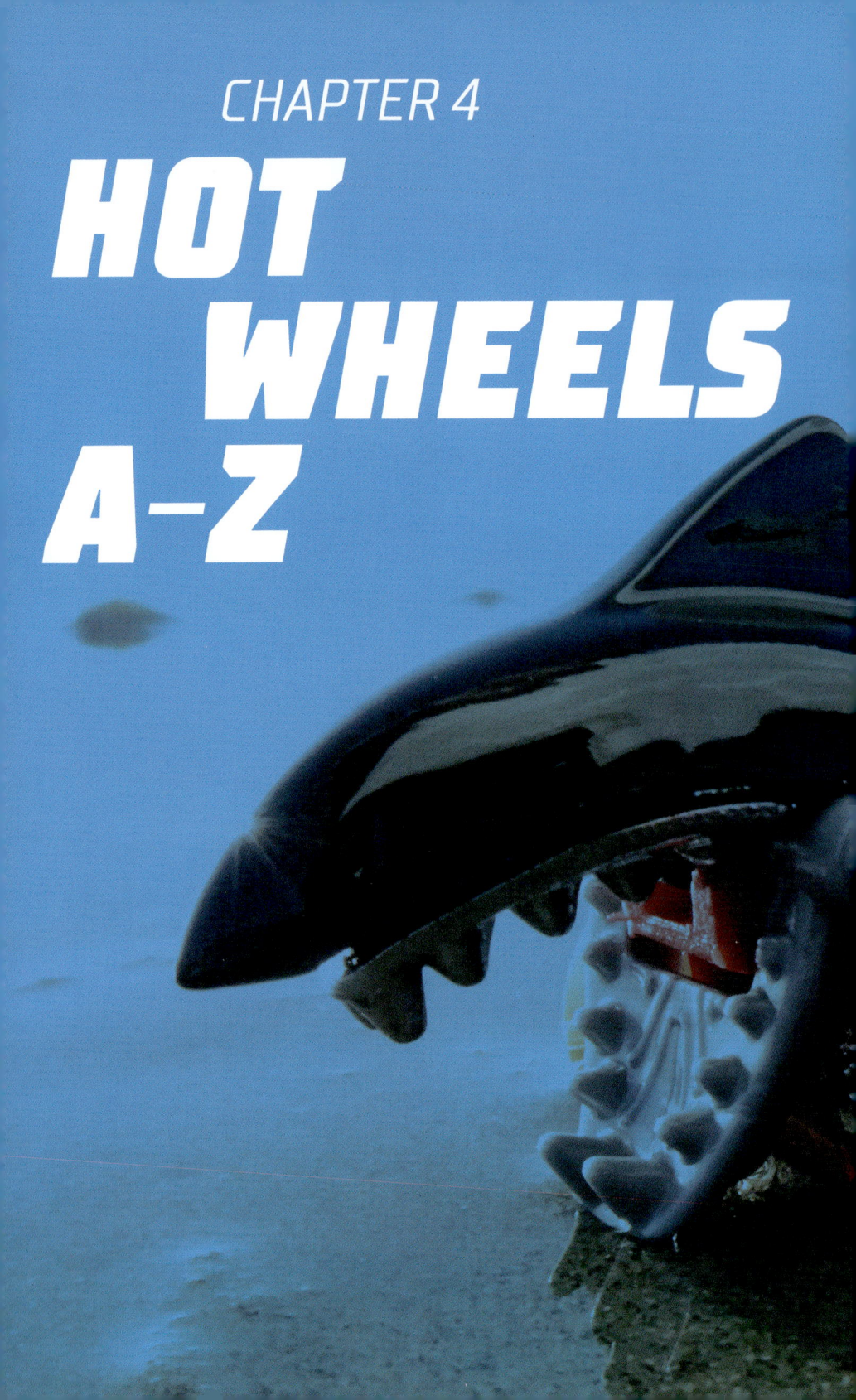

CHAPTER 4

HOT WHEELS A-Z

Get to know more than 160 original Hot Wheels designs! This section includes facts, stats, and tons of fascinating information about these unique creations that push boundaries in automotive design and purpose-built performance.

2JETZ

The 2JetZ was built along the lines of a Bonneville Salt Flats retro airplane belly tank racer with a futuristic flair. This unique concept and design have certainly earned its status as a legend. Did you know that the 2JetZ didn't start out as a toy? It began with a life-size, custom car.

The 2JetZ is inspired by a concept sketch of the "Face Peeler" from Hot Wheels designer Dwayne Vance.

HOT WHEELS
IN REAL LIFE

In celebration of the brand's 50th anniversary, Hot Wheels created the Legends Tour. The tour went to fifteen different cities and was on the hunt for incredible life-size custom cars made by fans. The 2JetZ was the first ever Legends Tour winner, establishing the creativity, originality, and garage spirit that make the tour so popular.

The life-size interior of the 2JetZ

The 2JetZ features a 627-horsepower engine and an actual vegetable steamer welded to the muffler for maximum thrust!

Born: 2019
2-TUFF

This HW Hot Truck is designed with a giant cargo bed that can haul it all! With its enormous and powerful V-8 engine, its shaped ridges that control the airflow over the hood and cab, and its sleek windshield, this urban truck can take you and your crew anywhere you want to go!

The 2-Tuff is tough enough that it earned a place in *Hot Wheels Let's Race*, the animated series.

AIN'T FARE

Slammed to the ground with drag-racing tires and twin diesel engines, this rodded-out bus will definitely get you from A to B faster than public transportation ever has before! The racing bucket seats allow passengers to ride comfortably, even at extreme speeds.

Born: 2018

AIRUPTION

This amazing machine spreads its wings and transforms into a fighter jet capable of supersonic speeds, both on and off the ground. With its aerodynamic design featuring two massive wings, the Airuption is always cleared for takeoff!

Born: 2017

AISLE DRIVER

This crazy, ride-on cart commands pole position at checkout. Load some figures in the basket and prepare for aisle-antics in a supermarket showdown. Will the Aisle Driver win the race?

Born: 2020

ALPHA PURSUIT

The Alpha Pursuit is the ultimate police vehicle for a futuristic world. The bad guys can run, but there's nowhere to hide when this sleek and speedy cruiser activates lights and sirens and joins in the chase.

ARISTO RAT

In a class of its own, this Legends of Speed car bulldozes its way to first place with its huge front spoiler, air scoop poking through the roof, and double twin-exhausts. Look closely and you'll spot a little rat inside carrying a wrench!

The Aristo Rat squeaked its way into the cast of *Hot Wheels Let's Race*.

Born: 2012

BAD TO THE BLADE

Known for its four-cylinder, turbocharged motorcycle engine and blistering speed, the Bad To The Blade was inspired by the concept of mixing a fighter jet with a dragon!

The Bad To The Blade cuts its way into *Hot Wheels Let's Race*.

HOT WHEELS
IN REAL LIFE

A life-size build of this car was first showcased during the Indy 500's 100th anniversary celebration.

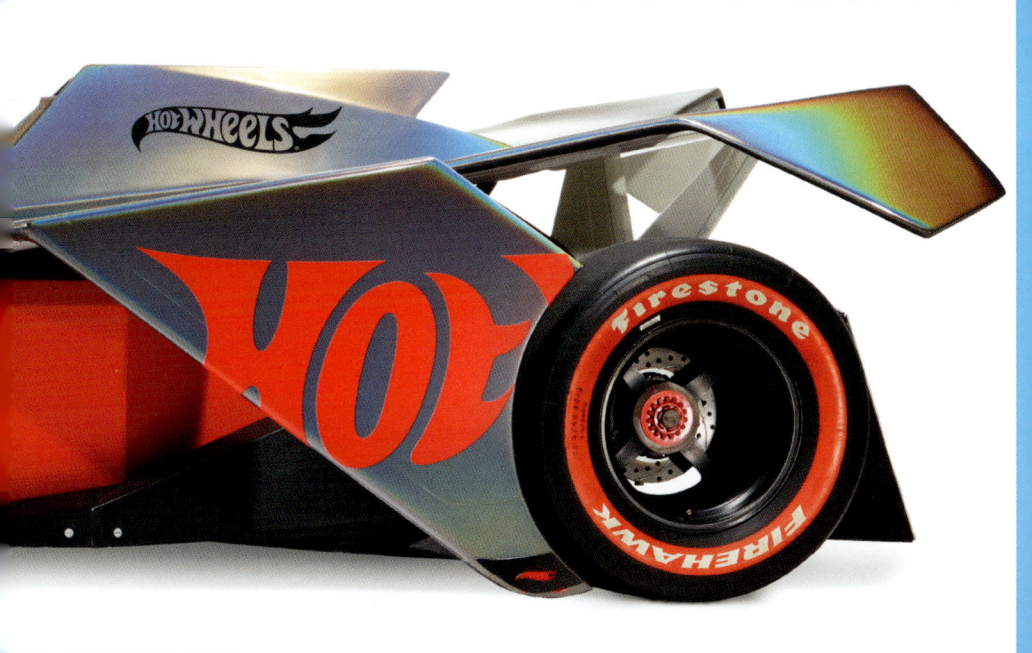

This real-life racer features a top speed of more than 230 miles per hour (mph)!

Born: 2023

BAJA BISON T5

Featuring a water-cooled battery system, high ground clearance, and a large windshield, this 4x4 racer is the future of electric off-roading. This EV (electric vehicle) is inspired by the prototype trucks used in T5 Cross-Country Rallying.

HOT WHEELS FACT

The first life-size Hot Wheels was the Twin Mill, built in 2001.

Born: 2017

BAJA HAULER

This HW Hot Truck features a formidable V-10, twin-turbo engine. With its eye-catching suspension, it can move colossal amounts of cargo across any terrain. No obstacle is too great for this powerful hauler!

HOT WHEELS FACT

#HotWheels is shared every thirty seconds on social media.

BAJA TRUCK

This off-track, desert racer with a custom, big-block engine can take on anything that comes its way. Though fully loaded with horsepower, it's surprisingly agile. Desert sand is no obstacle for this Hot Wheels truck!

NETFLIX

The Baja Truck soared its way into the cast of the animated series.

HOT WHEELS
IN REAL LIFE

In 2011, a custom Baja Truck jumped 332 feet in the air while going 100 miles per hour, breaking the previous record by thirty-one feet!

This real-life Baja Truck features a small-block, V-8 race engine and a suspension system flexible enough to accommodate any takeoff or landing. This off-track racer can go as fast as 140 miles per hour!

BARBIE DREAM CAMPER

Bringing Hot Wheels and Barbie together, this stylish RV (recreation vehicle) offers all the comforts of home as you go exploring. This spacious camper makes traveling a blast. Camping can be a dream when you have the perfect ride!

Dreaming of the many ways the Barbie Dream Camper can wow fans of both brands, Hot Wheels and Barbie designers put their imaginations together to transform this playset into a die-cast model.

BARBIE EXTRA

Grab a friend and ride top-down around town in this sparkly silver two-seat convertible with star-shaped headlights. The Barbie Extra car has scissor doors shaped like wings for a big entrance or exit. With comfy seats and "frunk" storage, this dream car is ready for as many outfit changes as needed!

Proving a smaller version can still be extra, the Hot Wheels design team added their star power to the Barbie Extra by creating a die-cast version of this Barbie convertible.

Born: 2018

BAZOOMKA

Inspired by a plane ride at the fair, this crazy ride-on features a pilot in the cockpit. This high-speeder is primed and ready to blast you off on the ride of your life!

Born: 2018

BEAT ALL

The rugged forest terrain may be tough, but the Beat All was built for the challenge. Featuring a segmented body, this beetle-inspired beast leaves the competition in the dust with its incredible endurance and formidable speed.

Born: 2018

BOGZILLA

Featuring a monstrous V-8 engine, this hill-jumping beast can take on any challenge. Its hefty tires and roll bar with a light rack enable this dune buggy to power through the summits all day and all night!

BONE SHAKER

A classic hot rod comes to life—or *afterlife*—in this stripped-down truck rod. The skull grille and skeleton hands around the headlights make it a menacingly frightening opponent. Perhaps no design embodies the Hot Wheels spirit as much as the Bone Shaker, one of the most popular Hot Wheels ever.

NETFLIX

The Bone Shaker is such an iconic Hot Wheels vehicle that an entire episode of *Hot Wheels Let's Race* is devoted to it.

HOT WHEELS
IN REAL LIFE

The Bone Shaker first came to life in 2011.

This 2019 real-life Bone Shaker has a sleek, chromed-out skull grille and a special paint job. It has a V-8 engine, 402 horsepower, and a top speed of 160 mph. The shifter even looks like a human spine!

Designer Larry Wood's 2006 Bone Shaker sketch

Born: 2017

BOOM CAR

Prepare for a blastoff with this explosive ride! The boom car is ready to catapult your mini figures outta this world with its rolling cannon. Are you ready to break some world records?

Born: 2018

BOT WHEELS

This high-tech, all-wheel-drive machine is primed and ready to attack! Packed with radar sensors and featuring a formidable laser cannon and autonomous-control drone, this super-fast cyborg is a real blast to drive!

Born: 2023

BRICK AND MOTOR

This hot rod is open-wheeled and can be customized for inventive racing. Use the removable front skull grille and dual-turbo engine to mix and match your ride and burn up the road with high-speed action!

Born: 2023

BRICKIN' DELIVERY

Keeping a "low profile" in its lowered van stance, this brick house of a vehicle is customizable, allowing you to create a new ride over time as you drive. Its removable and swappable brick body parts are compatible across the entire Brick Rides™ mini collection, allowing you to create a new ride every time you drive.

Born: 2022

BRICKING SPEED

Taking inspiration from vintage open-wheeled race cars, this brick car features a movable spoiler and driver. Use your bricks to design your own challenger and race to the finish line.

Born: 2022

BRICKING TRAILS

This interchangeable speeder is ready to roll. With its detachable roll cage and spare tire bumper, this off-roader will switch up for a completely new look!

BUBBLE MATIC

This Formula 1-style racer has a sci-fi-themed bubble hoop. The side pontoons are inspired by a soap bottle with a hoop inside, which can be flipped up for play. Pop some wheelies in this bubble blaster and it will tur-blow you away!

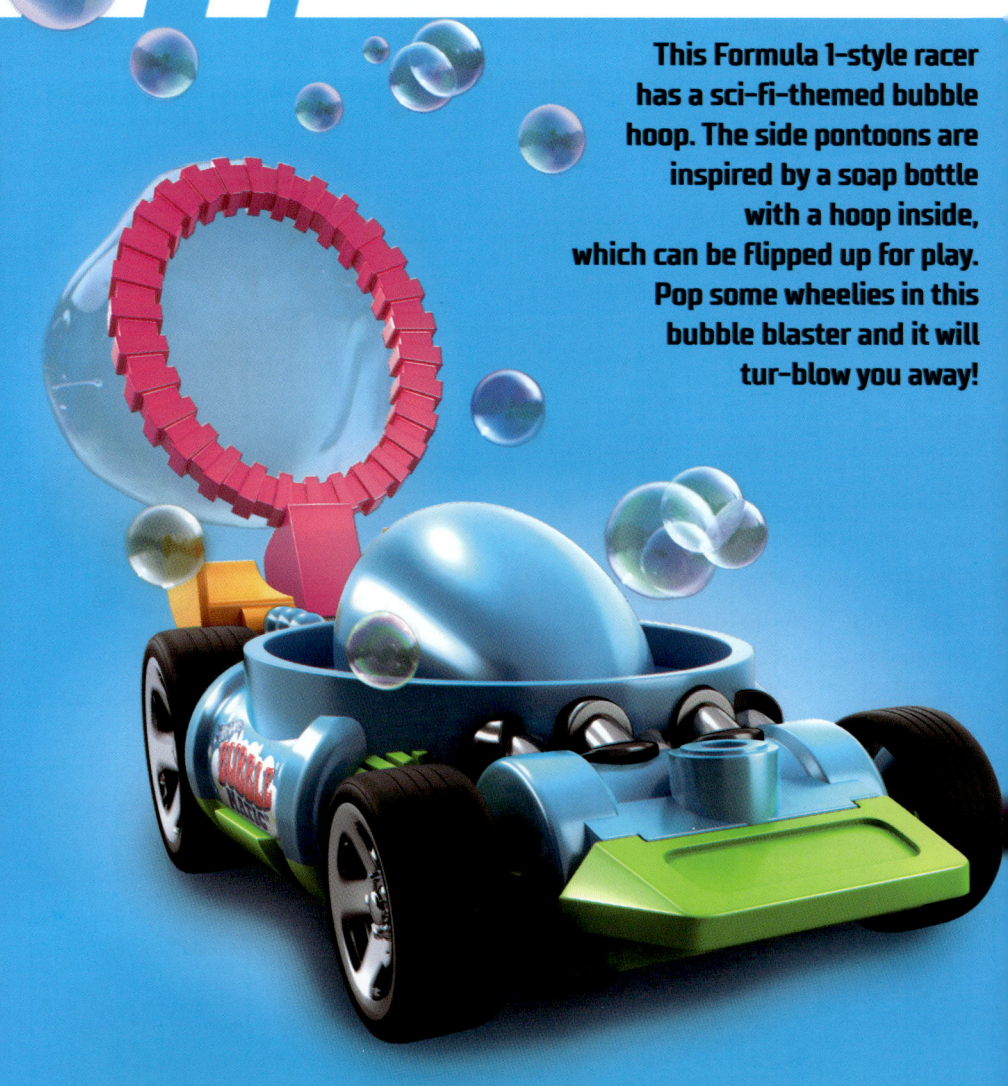

HOT WHEELS FACT

Hot Wheels is the best-selling toy in the world.*

*Reference: Circana

Born: 2018
BUNS OF STEEL

This fast-food competitor never plays *ketchup* and has all the trimmings to *relish* that first-place win. Featuring a massive burger on its back, french fries on the roof, soda cup exhaust pipes, and straws as a rear bumper, this sizzling rod serves up some hot competition! Take a look at the menu that's mounted on the door and order up something delicious!

NETFLIX

The Buns of Steel is a delicious addition to the animated series.

CAR-DE-ASADA

This supercharged ride is sure to spice things up on the road! The Car-De-Asada is a quirky, little hot rod that offers a tasty combination of speed and style. This car will burn past the competition at crunch time. With its fresh, taco-shaped body and rear wing of crispy nacho chips, your order is definitely up!

NETFLIX

The Car-De-Asada is on the menu!

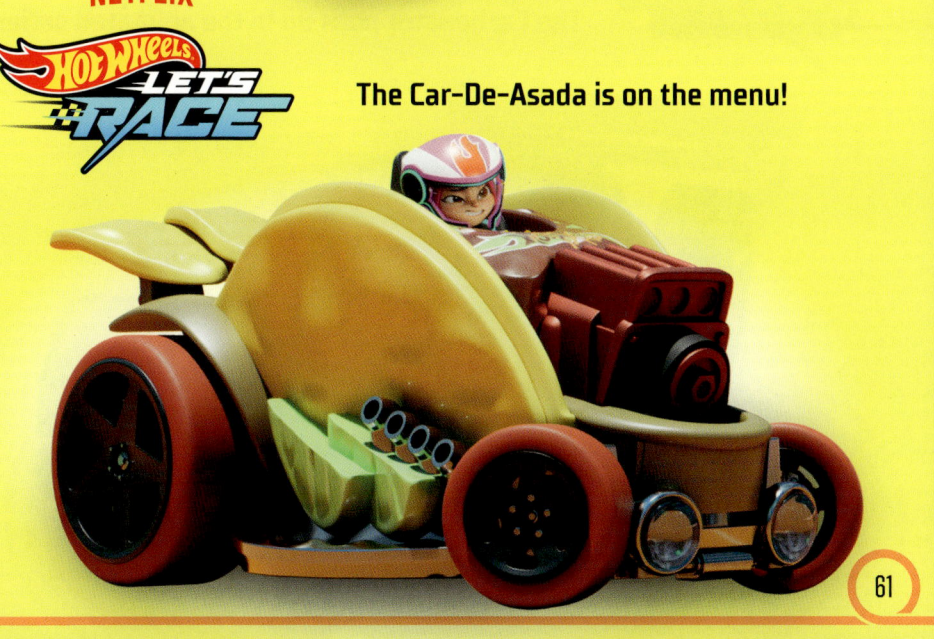

61

CARBONATOR

Shaped like a soda bottle with a huge rear wing and a turbine engine, this hot rod was made to "pop" your top.

NETFLIX

The Carbonator pops up in the animated series.

Born: 2023

CELERO GT

This racer is a combination of old romantic styling and modern aero technology. *Celero* means "to hurry" in Latin. With the power of a mid-mounted, fire-spitting engine, this impatient competitor will blaze a trail past its opponents on the track!

Born: 2020

CLIP ROD

Inspired by a money clip, this is a car you can carry anywhere. Designed with a Hot Wheels flame clip, it can be attached to a backpack or lunch bag—just in case you need to snack and roll!

COSMIC COUPE

This sci-fi movie-inspired Mars buggy is sure to impress. Both speedy and stylish, this planet-exploring coupe is the perfect ride to traverse unknown terrains.

COUNT MUSCULA

This impressive road-hugging muscle car is perfect for tearing up asphalt. Boasting a supercharger, a huge rear spoiler, and a big rear diffuser, this dragster packs some serious power!

Born: 2017

CRESCENDO

This luxury coupe is streamlined for maximum performance and features a stunning wrap-around glass canopy. With its twin-turbo, V-8 engine and curved body, it is the ultimate in style and power. Its aerodynamic shape built to cut through the air elevates this speedster to the next level.

Born: 2021

CUSTOM SMALL BLOCK

A great little car that is compatible with popular brick toys, this compact is totally customizable. The cab and engine can be removed to create the ultimate plug-and-play vehicle!

Born: 2018

CYBER SPEEDER

This high-tech, futuristic speedster features a flat-eight, twin-turbo engine and flip-up front chin spoiler for taking tight turns and killing those loops! With supercharged electric motors in each wheel, this super-intelligent car will drive you over the edge of reality!

Born: 2021

DAVANCENATOR

Inspired by the cyberpunk music movement of the 1980s, this car is a symbol of Hot Wheels's classic racing heritage. With a giant rear wing and front spoiler, this futuristic racer is powered by an engine fit for a Starfighter plane!

DEORA II

The modern version of this 1968 original features a bubble windshield, rear-mounted engine, and two surfboards—perfect for lazy summer "daze." Slinky curves, an integrated spoiler, and oval windows give the Deora II a sleek design update from the original.

NETFLIX

The Deora II is featured in the animated series.

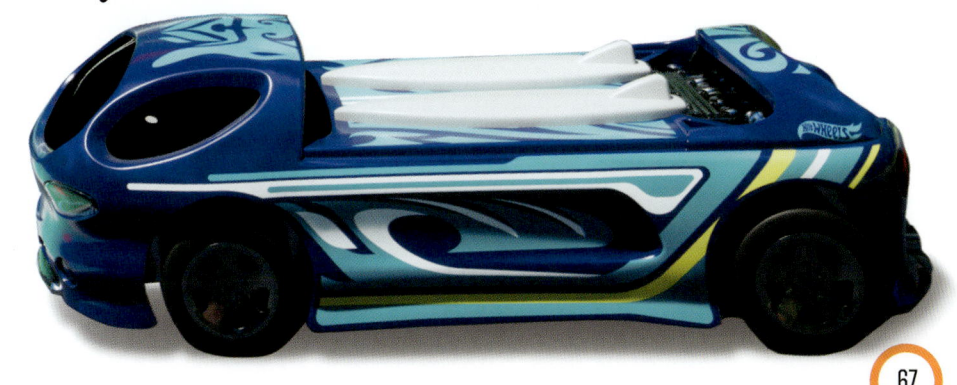

This 2003, real-life Deora II was built for the Hot Wheels 35th anniversary to pay tribute to the groundbreaking spirit and bold originality embodied by the Original Stunt Brand. The car featured a supercharged, 400+ horsepower engine and hit a top speed of 150 miles per hour!

This real-life Deora II cost $750,000 to build!

DEORA III

This version of the Deora is the third generation and uses electric power to get beach lovers to their happy place. Featuring twin surfboards to the rear, an awesome aero e-bike and a charging station, this cruiser is ready to shred some waves!

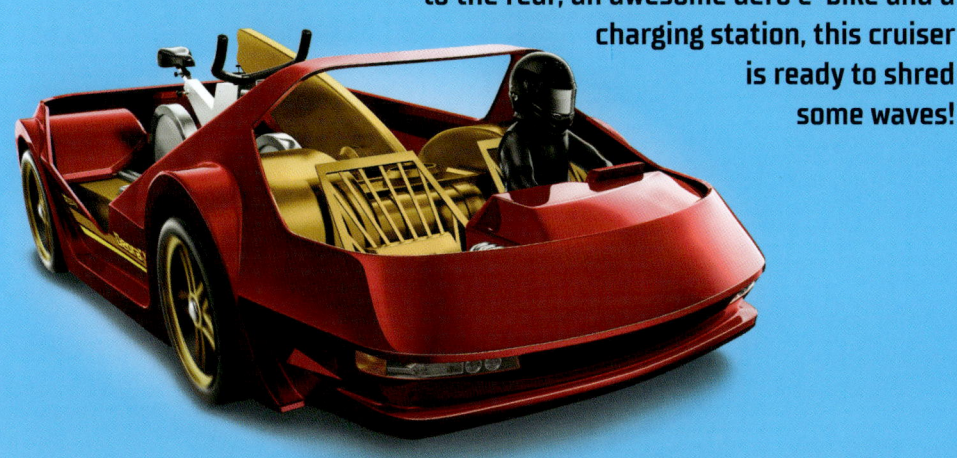

Born: 2023

DESSERT DRIFTER

This delicious drive puts pedal to the metal with an appetite for speed. Featuring a V-8 dragster and a roll cage, this hot-rodded car is a satisfyingly sweet ride.

Born: 2019

DIAPER DRAGGER

This bundle of joy packs a load of excitement! With a blown V-8 engine and super-wide rear slicks, you can't help but hear this baby roaring down the drag strip. Its baby bottle fuel tanks power this supercharged dragster to the next level!

Born: 2022

DIMACHINNI VELOCE

This four-seater coupe is Hot Wheels's take on the 1970s Italian sports car. It would slay the turns of the Rallye Sanremo. It's ready to shred asphalt or gravel.

DONUT DRIFTER

The Donut Drifter is a chocolate-frosted Fast Foodie that delivers on energy and performance. This sweet ride is low in drag and sprinkles fun as it races around the track.

The Donut Drifter is a sweet addition to the animated series.

73

Born: 2021

DRAFTNATOR

Inspired by NASCAR® trucks from the 1980s and '90s, this truck is track-ready and can even ride the loops. Featuring front and rear spoilers, a shiny V-8 engine, roll cage, and racing slicks, this racer is designed for two things: driving fast and turning left!

Born: 2023

DRAGGIN' WAGON

Hold on tight with this little wagon. It is mini-figure-compatible and more comfortable at a drag strip than out on a walk around the neighborhood. Put your pedal to the metal and leave the competition in the dust!

DRAGON BLASTER

With a scorching hot engine that will blast you from zero to sixty mph in three seconds, this medieval motor will breathe fire into the craziest of stunts!

HOT WHEELS FACT

Hot Wheels's birthday is celebrated on May 19th.

Born: 2024

DRIFT'N BREAK

Drift your cargo with style in this V-8-powered muscle car. Part wagon, part coupe, this all-performance mod is a shooting brake version of the legendary Fast Fish™.

Born: 2022

DRONE DUTY

Buckle up for a speedy rescue! This half-drone, half-car can detach and fly to any emergency on the track.

Born: 2020

DUCK N' ROLL

This quirky Street Beast is certainly unique. When conditions get bad, this unusual-looking hot rod will leave all the other contestants standing flat-footed. Time to release the quackin' . . .

NETFLIX

The Duck N' Roll is featured in the animated series.

77

Born: 2018
DUNE DADDY

This extreme off-roader features a giant wheel carrier on top and a rugged utility bar with three mounted lights. Its fearsome five-liter, turbo-charged V-6 engine kicks out 368 horsepower and 459 foot-pounds of torque. The four-wheel drive system enables it to both scale the summits and roar by the shores!

Born: 2018
DUNE-A-SOAR

A prototype for a single-seater hybrid competition machine, the Dune-A-Soar is the buggy to beat. Featuring outrageous suspension and side scoops for optimal airflow, this all-American, speedy off-roader will make all the competition extinct! The mega candle-power lights, lasers, and LiDAR range fenders allow the driver to maintain pace during dark hours.

EL SEGUNDO COUPE

Incorporating 1960s grand-tourer (GT) styling, this coupe's design is inspired by a keychain—and can be used as one! You'll be burning rubber in no time with this second model of the iconic Coupe Clip™ that features wheels!

Born: 2017

EL VIENTO

This high-performance concept car captures the future of driving. It has a low-drag design and aerodynamic body, so it literally rides like the wind. It also features a clear canopy which can be taken off to expose the detailed interior of this striking hybrid.

Born: 2018

ELECTRAK

This high-tech hybrid X-Raycer features a twin-turbo, ten-cylinder combustion engine and two electric motors that really send it charging to the front of the race! High-power battery packs provide the energy for phenomenal acceleration. The competition won't know *watt* hit them!

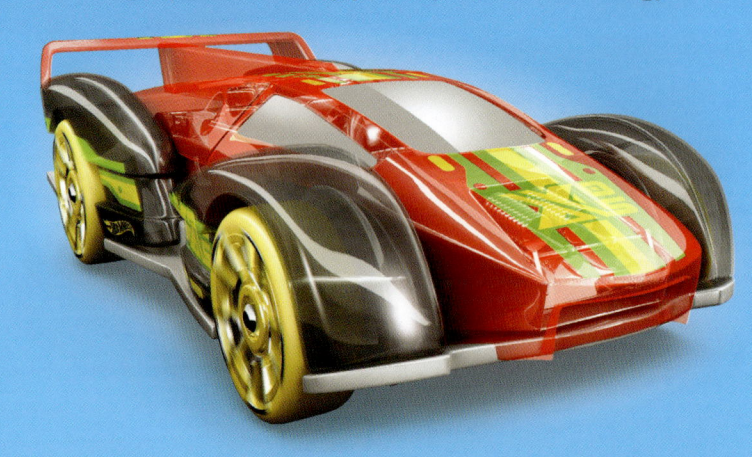

Born: 2019

ELECTRO SILHOUETTE

This eco-friendly endurance racer is the new breed of speed! Equipped with a powerful electric motor and a tilting chin spoiler to take on the highest loops, the future of auto racing has never looked so good!

EMOTICAR

This car gives you all the feels . . . on wheels! Its body resembles a racing helmet, and it has faces and expressions sculpted into the front, back, top, and bottom. Get in motion with oodles of emotion—then grab a marker and express your feelings on the blank spots!

Born: 2020

ERIKENSTEIN ROD

Named after its designer, this hot rod truck is built to haul something . . . but it ain't cargo. Slammed to the ground, wide-bodied, with a roll cage and a blown engine, this rod can easily take on the competition!

Born: 2018
EXOTIQUE

This mid-engine, exotic car features a 700-horsepower, V-12 engine that will obliterate any opponent! With enhanced hardware and sleek lines, this distinctive ride sounds good in any language.

Born: 2018
FAST MASTER

This elegant challenger offers speed and style with every mile! Featuring an immense trunk and five-liter, V-10, 500-horsepower engine, this first-class racer is the master of performance and luxury.

FLASH DRIVE

With a 1,000-horsepower engine, the Flash Drive will blast you into the future faster and sleeker than you could have ever imagined! This cutting-edge, four-wheel-drive features an energy storage system charged by both the engine and the regenerative braking system. It has front and rear wings that can be raised or lowered, modifying the downforce and clearance for track.

Born: 2024

FLIPPIN FAST

This adaptable automobile can be driven in so many ways, making it one of the most versatile vehicles on the road. Flip it, spin it, and even drive it upside down for that unique experience on the track.

Born: 2020

FORWARD FORCE

A true performance car, the Forward Force is designed with racing and stunting on Hot Wheels's iconic orange track in mind. With interior details—which can be seen through the clear canopy—and an electric motor, this supercharged dynamo energizes the track!

Born: 2021

FUSIONBUSTA

A super-powered beast designed for optimum performance, this rod is not one to mess with. Featuring a hood scoop towering over the body, it can look down at the other competitors as it rolls unchallenged through streets of the future!

GAZELLA R

Equipped with a twin-turbo engine, this speedster features an oversized rear wing and an active chin spoiler for unstoppable performance as it takes on the loops! With its streamlined, aerodynamic body and opaque side windows, this rewired Gazella GT™ will totally knock your socks off!

Born: 2020

GEOTERRA

This awesome ride is inspired by off-road automotive culture. Handling extreme terrain with the precision and speed of a track car, the Geoterra will blaze its trailway beyond where the road ends!

Born: 2022

GLORY CHASER

A celebration of a 1950s GT masterpiece, the design of this classic would fit right in at the Mille Miglia and Le Mans races. This roadster features an exposed engine, sleek racing silhouette, hugging wheels, and the right DNA to enter any competition!

The Glory Chaser is featured in the animated series.

GOTTA GO

This compact little dump truck certainly keeps things moving in style. When you're on the go, sometimes you just *gotta go*! With six bathroom details including a toilet-themed license plate holder, and a toilet seat that actually moves up and down, this truck rolls! This ride will leave you looking flushed!

NETFLIX

The Gotta Go wipes out the competition in *Hot Wheels Let's Race*.

89

Born: 2020

GRAND CROSS

This functional crossover car embraces comfort and speed—and it delivers on both counts. Whether you need to go to the mall or the mountains, this sleek ride will get you there with style and performance.

Born: 2023

GROUP C FANTASY

This version of a Group C-compliant, single-seat race car is certainly a champion on the track. With a ferocious mid-mounted, V-8 engine and push-rod suspension, this speedster will always finish first!

GRUPPO X24

A modern interpretation of a classic Le Mans sports car, this prototype racer is built for twenty-four-hour endurance. Its long stabilizer keeps it glued to the track, and the wrap-around windscreen gives an amazing range of vision for the driver.

HOT WHEELS FACT

Hot Wheels are sold in over 150 countries.

GT-SCORCHER

Inspired by the cool Group 5 racers of the 1980s and '90s, this fire-breathing beast is ready to rumble! With its wide body, active chin spoiler, clear headlamps, and massive rear wing, this racer is geared up to take on the competition!

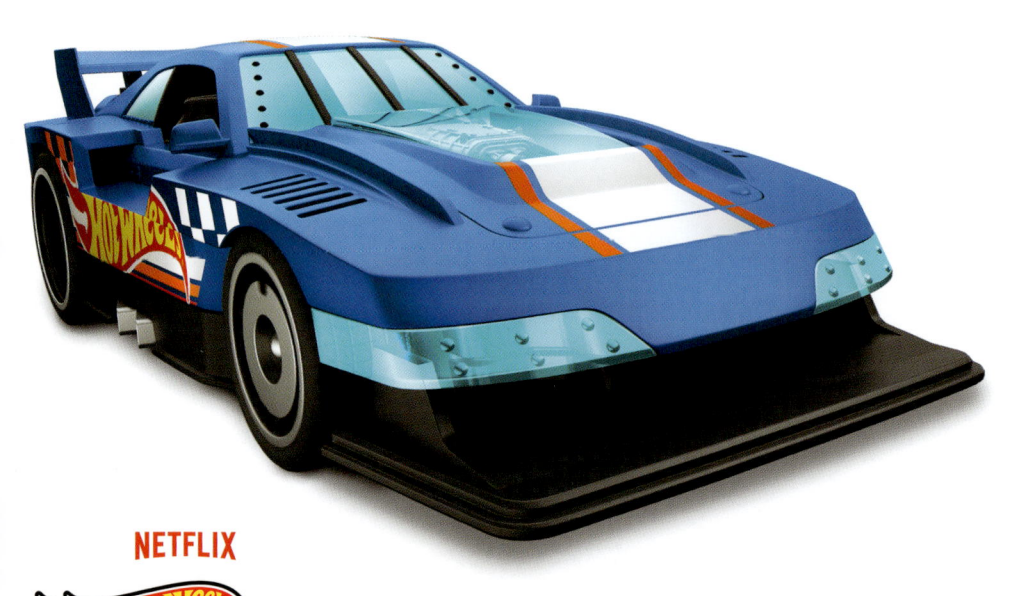

NETFLIX

The GT-Scorcher is one of the hottest cars featured in the animated series.

Born: 2019

HAUL-O-GRAM

This futuristic truck is designed with the legendary Hot Wheels orange track in mind. This awesome truck will rocket through the loops to the finish line with its V-16, twin-turbo engine, adjustable front spoiler, and a wind-cheating aero cab.

Born: 2021

HEAD GASKET

This hot rod will blow your mind! The Head Gasket is designed to get ahead of the competition. Tighten your chin strap and get your head on straight because this brain burner is Hot Wheelin'!

Born: 2017

HEAD STARTER

This vintage race vehicle in Tooned style sprints onto the track with a three-liter, V-8 engine. This thrill-seeker reaches speeds that will make your head wobble!

Born: 2019

HEAVY HITCHER

An ideal hookup, this truck can tow any stranded cars around Hot Wheels City. With its double arm, gigantic V-8 engine, and enormous push bumper, the Heavy Hitcher can sweep any broken-down vehicle off the highway.

HI BEAM

This high-performance rally car has a ground clearance tall enough to take on all the bumps and jumps around the track. With a 600-horsepower engine, this off-roader is a powerful force to be reckoned with!

Born: 2022

HOT WIRED

This aggressively styled racer with massive e-motors (electric motors) and modern tech brings drag racing into the modern age.

HOTWEILER

This Street Beast is chomping at the bit to guard the neighborhood with its unstoppable fur-ocity. With a powerful engine and modified five-spoke wheels on the front axle providing jaw-moving action, this canine racer sure does pack a bite!

HOT WHEELS FACT

Hot Wheels debuted in 1968 with sixteen cars.

HOVER & OUT

This unique ride is the future of driving—and flying! With its powerful dual jets and two propellers—one in the front and one in the back—this awesome vehicle can fly through and above traffic.

Born: 2023

HW-4-TRAC

Originally sporting the Hot Wheels 55th Anniversary Race Team livery, this open-wheel racer hits the track and pushes the boundaries of speed. The wings and winglets generate a superior downforce while speeding through loops and banked curves. This racer will blast past the competition to victory!

Born: 2018

HW50

A modern take on a vintage hot rod, this commemorative 50th Anniversary vehicle is a collector's must-have! Sitting low to the ground with a big-bore, V-10 engine, this dragster can really burn some rubber. With a roof hatch for climbing in and out of the cockpit, this American racer will leave the competition standing on the strip.

Born: 2023

HW BRAILLE RACER - TWIN MILL

This special speedster is designed specifically for people who read Braille. "Twin Mill," "68," and "Hot Wheels" are displayed in Braille on the body surface for an inclusive play experience.

Born: 2024

HW ULTIMATE T-REX TRANSPORTER

Modeled after the Ultimate T-Rex Transporter, this 1:64-scale die-cast version of the hauler features T-Rex jaw power and a protective top. Buckle up and tear through the streets with maximum velocity and ferocity!

NETFLIX

The hauler roars to life and propels the kid racers on a high-speed chase in the animated series.

Born: 2020

HW WARP SPEEDER

This single-driver track racer delivers the ultimate speed and performance. Designed for pulling stunts on the iconic orange Hot Wheels track, the top surface of this car features a wing, allowing for maximum grip as it rip-roars its way to victory!

Born: 2019

HYPER ROCKER

This seriously powerful off-roader can tackle even the bumpiest obstacle in its path thanks to its working suspension and black fenders. This futuristic truck is seriously heavy-duty!

Born: 2019

i-BELIEVE

Inspired by extraterrestrial films, this vehicle showcases a design in the genre of science fiction. Featuring a hard-shell exoskeleton that surrounds and shields its alien pilot, this faster-than-light sports car can take on any space invasion!

Born: 2018

KICK KART

This ride-on is a souped-up speed kart that delivers optimum performance. Combining a jet engine with a combustion engine, this hybrid-powered go-kart is ready to kick things off!

LAYIN' LOWRIDER

This lowrider features a high nose and a tilted stance. The powerful tremble of this hot rod is sure to draw attention!

LETHAL DIESEL

With its body slammed to the ground and its chopped and angled roof, this is one rod you don't want to mess with. Designed with attitude, aggressive lines, and a supercharged chrome V-8 engine that juts out of the hood, this earthquake of a ride will roar along the track and shake your bones!

LIGHTNIN' BUG

Inspired by the iconic dune buggies of the 1960s, this modern-day racer is the coolest buggy around. With cargo space under the hood and an exposed rear engine, you can totally "bug out" in this ride.

LIMITED GRIP

Drift the day away with this truck's twin-turbo, V-8 engine and bash bar that's built to shield it from any collision. Practice makes perfect vehicle control with its hand-controlled rear brakes that allow it to slide sideways, make smoke, and burn rubber on the tracks.

Born: 2020

LINDSTER PROTOTYPE

This ground-hugging racer, named after its designer, is a mini collector's favorite. It will blast its way around the track thanks to the rear mid-engine prototype and the covered rear wheels for improved aerodynamics that help it fly down the straightaways and make ground-sticking turns.

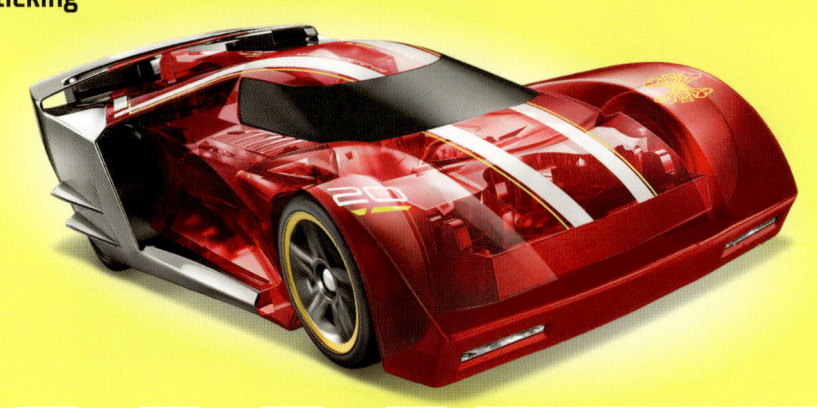

Born: 2022

LOLUX

This mid-engine racing pickup is designed to tear up the track with style and ease. With its large wings, low stance, aero kit, and dragster tires, this truck has real racing spirit!

LOOP COUPE

With a suspension designed to withstand an intense amount of force, this all-wheel-drive Thrill Racer features a six-speed transmission and a turbocharged, four-cylinder engine.

HOT WHEELS FACT

There are over 130 new car designs introduced each year.

HOT WHEELS IN REAL LIFE

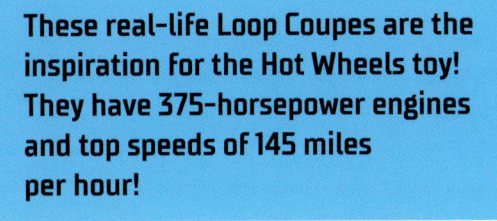

These real-life Loop Coupes are the inspiration for the Hot Wheels toy! They have 375-horsepower engines and top speeds of 145 miles per hour!

The two Loop Coupes set a Guinness World Record in the 2012 X Games when they defied gravity and completed the Hot Wheels Double Dare Loop stunt!

To prepare, the drivers practiced loops and inversions in stunt planes. Both cars successfully navigated a loop the size of a six-story building!

MACH IT GO

This Hot Wheels original is a take on a vintage IMSA®
(International Motor Sports Association) racer powered
by a modern jet. This single-seat racer has large side intakes
to flow air to the jet engine, taking this set of wheels exactly
where they need to be!

HOT WHEELS FACT

*Over eight billion Hot Wheels have been
produced since 1968.*

Born: 2018

MACH SPEEDER

From the side scoops designed to feed the air to its twin-turbo, V-6 hybrid engine driving the rear wheels and electric motors driving the front ones, this powerful machine is built for endurance. Resembling a wide-mouth predator fish, the Mach Speeder makes a mockery of the competition!

NETFLIX

The Mach Speeder is featured in the animated series.

Born: 2012

MAD MANGA

This anime-inspired speedster features an aggressive long-nose, chin spoiler, and over-fenders. The front-mounted oil cooler and extended exhaust pipes are for both high performance and for makin' a lot of noise late at night.

The Mad Manga is featured in *Hot Wheels Let's Race*.

MANGA TUNER

A tribute to manga culture, this kawaii ride is a collector's dream. Transport yourself to the next chapter of tuner culture and ride through the streets of Tokyo in style!

HOT WHEELS FACT

Over 500 million Hot Wheels are produced per year.

Born: 2020

MATTEL DREAM MOBILE

The Mattel Dream Car debuted in 1953, fifteen years before the creation of Hot Wheels! To commemorate Mattel's 75th anniversary, Hot Wheels released this die-cast version of the futuristic, bubble-topped convertible.

The original toy from 1953

Born: 2022

MAX STEEL

This single-seater speeder is truly unique in design. Featuring a low, air-cooled, flat-six engine, this highboy hot rod is one of a kind!

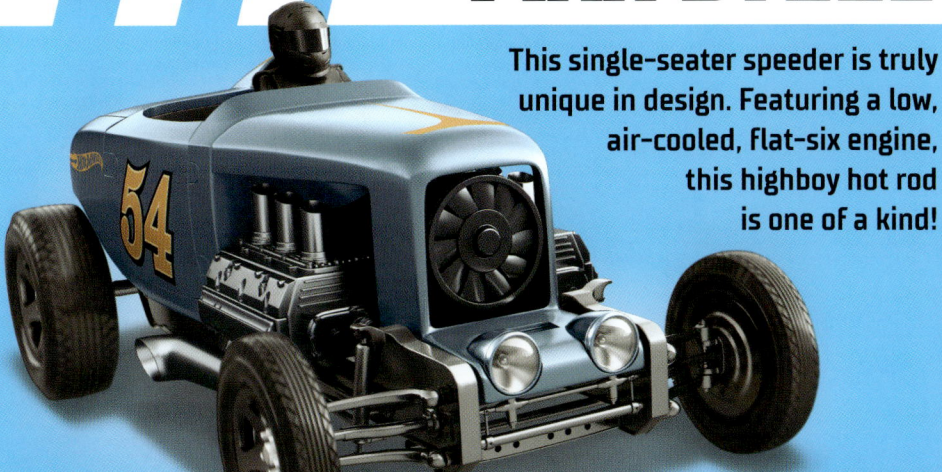

Born: 2022

MIGHTY K

Inspired by the Japanese mini kei truck, this ride is small yet mighty! Versatile and compact with baby proportions, this truck may look small, but don't underestimate its power . . . k?

Born: 2019

MOD ROD

This modified classic hot rod contains a powerful V-6 engine and massive ram air system. With its panoramic front windshield, this design will definitely become a collector's favorite!

Born: 2023

MOD SPEEDER

First, there was Muscle, then there was Project, and now there is Mod. The iconic family of speeders has a new addition with the latest, full-blown, customized version with a huge front diffuser and ducktail spoiler. This speeder is always race-ready!

Born: 2024

MONSTER HIGH GHOUL MOBILE

This *creeperific* car, covered in spiderwebs, is perfect for those spooky-fun midnight rides! Featuring an engine that drives so smoothly, you'll think you're floating on vampire wings. This car is the *skulltimate* ride to *fang out* with your boos!

The Hot Wheels designers proved they were too *ghoul* for school when they *screamed* up with the Monster High designers to create a Hot Wheels version of the Ghoul Mobile.

MO-STASH

This land speeder is an open-top two-seater with extra-long side exhausts. Setting new records with style, this fashionable motor even has a hidden flick mustache.

Born: 2017

MOTOSAURUS

This Street Beast may appear smaller than the other dinos, but it's no primeval pushover! Featuring characteristic back plates and a low-to-the-ground profile for taking those corners with speed and precision, this spiked speedster will dominate the track for ages to come!

MOTO WING

Inspired by a cyberpunk girl named Jiro in Japan, this track hero makes for a truly sinister ride. A fighter plane and motorcycle mash-up, this ride features a huge wing for stability, a massively modded two-stroke motorcycle engine, hybrid dynamos, and a chain drive.

Born: 2021

MUSCLE AND BLOWN

This roadster combines the classic lines of a muscle car and "rods" it out. With a velocity-stack-intake manifold, body-side exhausts, dual-pass radiator, fender flairs, and racing slicks, it's the perfect track weapon!

Born: 2019

MUSCLE BOUND

A take on a 1970s muscle car, this speedster struggles to contain its enormous power. The twin, four-barrel, V-8 engine in this gas-guzzler is so massive a huge bulge had to be built into the hood just to contain it!

Born: 2016

MUSCLE SPEEDER

With an oversized, supercharged V-8 engine roaring under the exposed hood window, this classic muscle car has an extra serving of torque. This power giant is built to last!

HOT WHEELS FACT

The most expensive Hot Wheels toy ever sold was the Beach Bomb™ for $72,000!

Born: 2020

PIXEL SHAKER

This ride-on is inspired by eight-bit video games and modeled on other iconic Hot Wheels castings, like the Mountain Mauler™ and Bone Shaker. Nothing will block the way for this pixelated power racer!

Born: 2014

PROJECT SPEEDER

This recently rescued muscle car is definitely a work in progress. Under the dents and dirt is a supercharged V-8 engine with an extra serving of torque. After some serious restoration work, this sleeping giant is sure to roar once more!

Born: 2024

PUNK ROD

Featuring a powerful, V-8 mid-engine, carbon fiber aero, mohawk intake, and swan-neck rear wing, this super-challenger is a hot-rodded masterpiece!

Born: 2017

QUAD ROD

This moto boasts an impressive suspension capable of coping with those monumental jumps. It's a quad rod that features a 500-cc (cubic capacity) pushrod motorcycle motor and toothy, off-road tires for maximum grip. Hold on tight and enjoy the ride!

RAIJIN EXPRESS

Dekotora are highly decorated trucks that have been in Japan since the 1970s. Featuring Raijin, the god of thunder, lightning, and storms, this express truck brings it all together in explosive detail!

Born: 2021

RALLY BAJA CRAWLER

This extreme off-road beast has a wide body and an overwhelming stance. It's full of spy gear and monstrous performance! No obstacle stands in the way of this mechanical monster!

Born: 2017

RALLY CAT

A road car turned into a tarmac fighter, the Rally Cat features wings with a very wide stance and lots of intakes and vents for air to feed and cool off that impressive engine. This Daredevil is a fur-midable opponent, chasing its prey as it zooms from out of nowhere and pounces on the finish line.

Born: 2022

RALLY SPECIALE

Inspired by the Italian rally cars of the 1970s, this mid-engine racer has a short wheelbase for improved agility and a sharp, modern body with old-school rally details. Outfitted with retro-influenced spotlights and taillights, this vehicle brings some vintage flair to rally racing.

RIG HEAT

This sleek European racing rig is a mean contender. Its distinctive, aerodynamic tear-shaped cab with two modern wings directs air toward the side spoilers and around the colossal engine. A low, wide, and formidable big rig, it rip-roars its way to the front of the field.

HOT WHEELS FACT

Hot Wheels makes over 6,000 miles of orange track each year.

129

Born: 2014

RIP ROD

Reaching top speeds upwards of 125 mph, this ripper's got some kick. With fang-like exhaust tips and a mask for a grille, it's a creature you don't want to mess with.

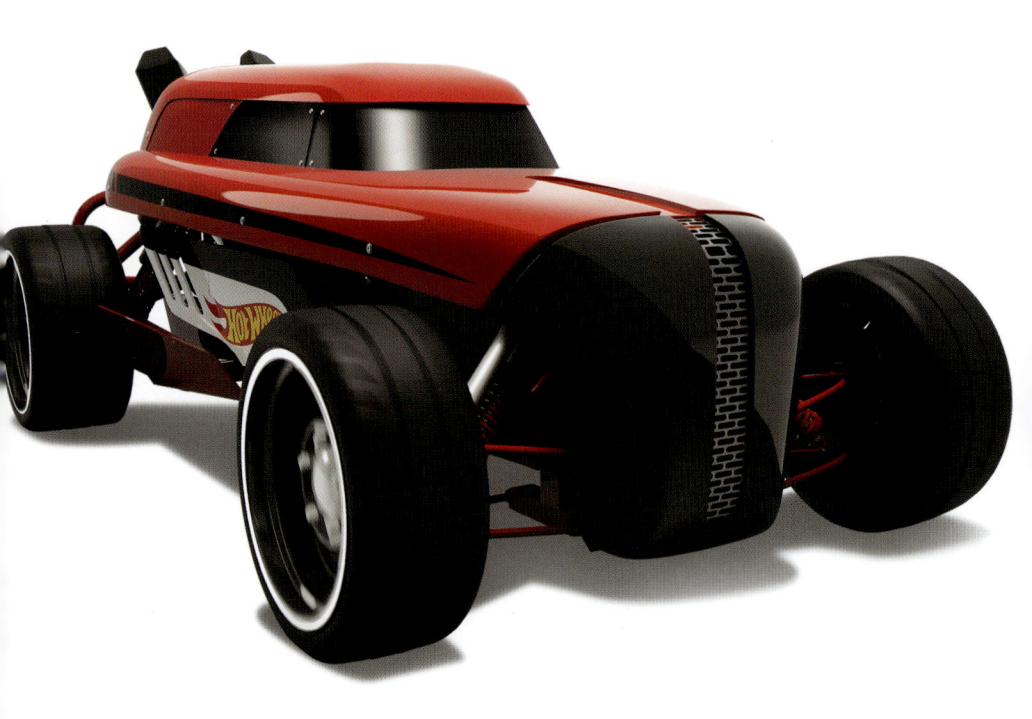

HOT WHEELS FACT

The largest Hot Wheels collection is worth over one million dollars.

HOT WHEELS
IN REAL LIFE

The black, real-life model, affectionately known as the "Red Ripper," is outfitted with a 900-cc Polaris engine and performs a backflip on the live-action web series *Hot Wheels World's Best Driver.*

This blue, real-life Rip Rod has a one-liter, 200-horsepower engine, a four-cylinder motor, and a top speed of 125 miles per hour! This rod can go from zero to sixty in three seconds!

Born: 2018

RISE 'N CLIMB

Designed for the serious cyclist to blaze some trails, this sporty, two-door racer with space for bicycles in the back adds off-road flavor to its on-road performance! Inspired by speedy coupes and hooked-up hybrids, this modern electric crossover will rise to any challenge!

Born: 2018

RISING HEAT

This super-fast rally vehicle is inspired by hill-climbing, time-attack race cars. Featuring massive front and rear wings, a mid-engine mount, and a sweet set of pipes, this agile diehard racer packs some serious downforce. Flip up the front spoiler to clear loops on the iconic orange track!

ROAD BANDIT

This eye-catching bus is inspired by the colorful jeepneys driven in the Philippines. With its V-8 engine, this supercharged bandit will get you to your destination fast!

Born: 2022

ROADSTER BITE

Inspired by a viper snake, this modern, single-seat convertible roadster has the aerodynamics of a jet fighter, making it one dangerous contender! Featuring an exposed engine and fang flaps up front, this predator will take out the competition with one bite.

Born: 2008

ROCKETFIRE

This rocket-powered lunar racer will make you the fastest car on the moon. Built entirely around a rocket booster, this moon machine is made for the space race. Aileron guides, airless tires, and gravity-feed fuel pods give the Rocketfire all the boost it needs to make it out of this world.

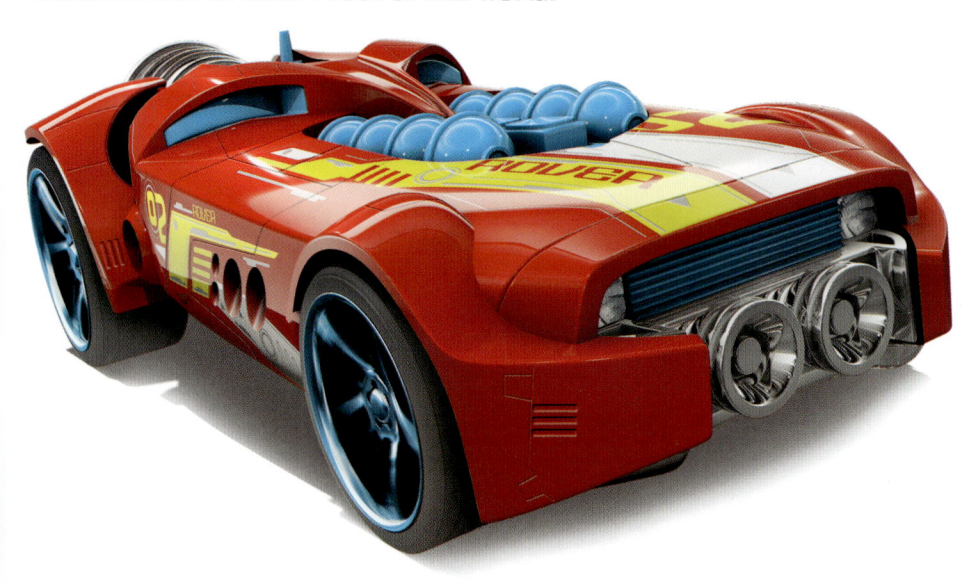

NETFLIX

The Rocketfire burns up the track in the animated series.

Born: 2022

ROCKIN' RAILER

Taking inspiration from rail dragsters of the 1960s, this speedster goes from zero to 100 to in 0.8 seconds! Featuring an exposed front engine, the driver sits between the rear wheels to provide better traction.

Born: 2020

ROCKIN' SANTA SLED

This sled is anything but silent on Christmas Eve. Santa ditches the reindeer for some superb horsepower. Featuring a figurine in the cockpit which moves back and forth as it rolls along, Santa will rock this ride through the night!

Born: 1974

RODGER DODGER

Hot Wheels meets muscle with this big-motor racer. The long hood, broad shoulders, and blown engine let you know it means business.

NETFLIX

This Hot Wheels legend muscled its way onto the animated series.

RODGER DODGER 2.0

This iconic monster delivers tons of torque via four electric motors—one powering each wheel! A next-generation version of the original Rodger Dodger, this muscle car rockets from zero to sixty in 1.2 seconds and tops out at 374 miles per hour!

HOT WHEELS FACT

Ten million Hot Wheels are produced every week.

Born: 2021

RODGER DODGER (MAGIC 8 BALL)

This magical monster combines the Hot Wheels Rodger Dodger and Mattel's entertaining Magic 8 Ball toy. Riding this muscle car is an absolute joy with its sleek, black paint job and Magic 8 Ball symbol on the doors. Featuring iconic phrases such as "ask again later," "without a doubt," and "reply hazy try again"— "all signs point to yes" when this racer is on the road!

ROLLER TOASTER

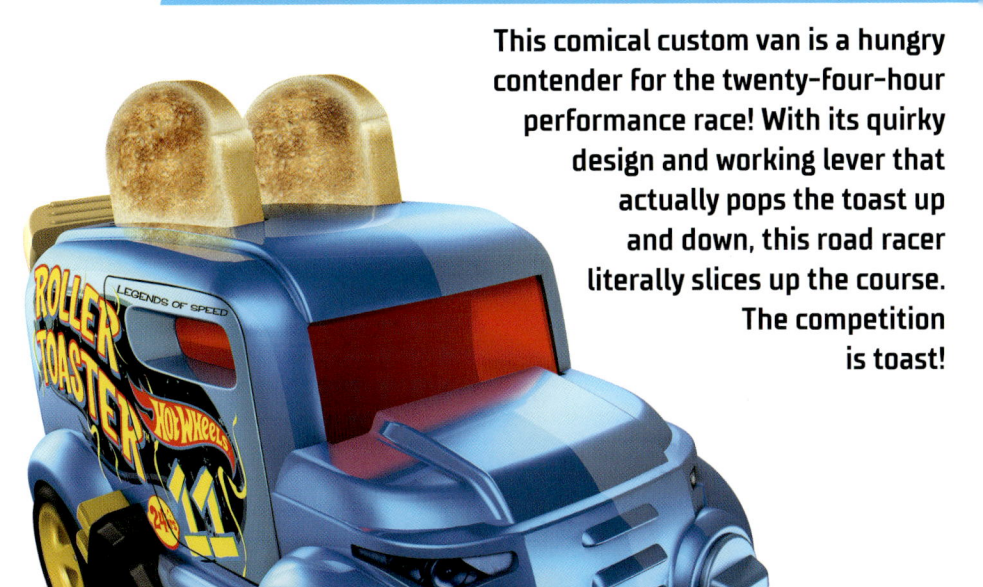

This comical custom van is a hungry contender for the twenty-four-hour performance race! With its quirky design and working lever that actually pops the toast up and down, this road racer literally slices up the course. The competition is toast!

The Roller Toaster springs into action in the animated series.

ROLLIN' SOLO

The Rollin' Solo is a futuristic racer designed for speed on the famed orange track. This autonomous robo-racer is a worthy challenger. Launch or boost it to see it fly through the loops with ease!

Born: 2019

RUNWAY RES-Q

With a nod to science fiction, this vehicle with aerodynamic contouring will beat any racer to the tarmac to save the day! It features a hinged rescue nozzle to squirt safety foam so the jets can land safely on the runway.

Born: 2020

RV THERE YET

This combination car and camper is designed for adventure. Perfect for long weekends away, the sturdy RV There Yet has a metal camper and will go wherever the road may take you.

Born: 2021

SAND BURNER

This fully prepped rally machine is up to any challenge. When there are miles of tire-splitting, oil-pan-busting terrain between you and the finish line, this off-roader will burn through the competition and scatter the ashes!

Born: 2018

SANDIVORE

This single-seater, off-road racer has style and attitude. It can devour dunes for dinner with its impressive six-cylinder, mid-engine layout and high ground clearance. There's no messing with this hungry challenger!

Born: 2021

SEE ME ROLLIN'

Just roll with it! This exciting little vehicle is custom-built and has a secret feature: a huge rolling wheel shows one chosen number through the roof display. Let's hope your lucky number comes up!

SHARK BITE

Just when you think it's safe to get back on the road, along comes the Shark Bite! With jaws that chomp as it rolls, this mechanical Street Beast is the ultimate track predator!

NETFLIX

The Shark Bite is featured in the animated series.

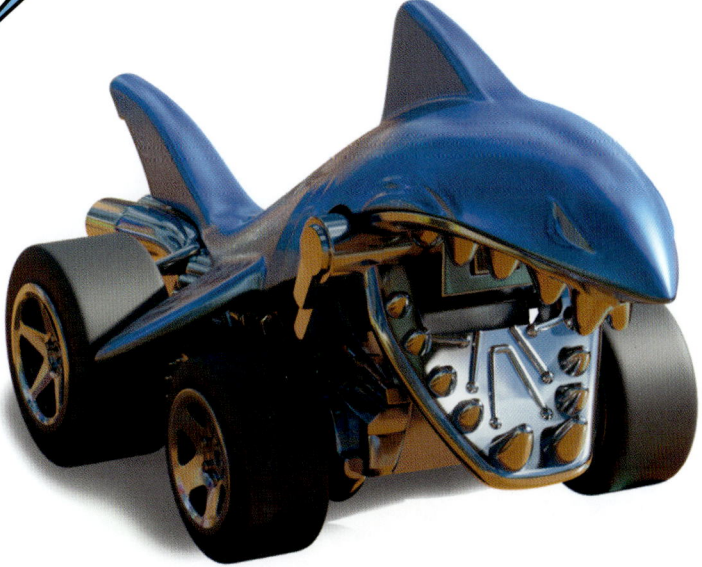

Born: 2010

SKULL CRUSHER

Featuring bone-rattling acceleration, a ribcage roll cage, and an exposed spinal cord with six intakes, this hot rod is ready to give you the ultimate lesson in vehicle anatomy.

NETFLIX

The Skull Crusher is featured in *Hot Wheels Let's Race*.

SKULL SHAKER

This trailblazer really shakes things up on the track. Featuring a bobblehead that moves as the wheels rotate and chrome exhaust pipes to help it cool off, the Skull Shaker has a bone to pick with its rivals and will fracture every speed record!

Born: 2017

SKY DOME

This aerodynamic vehicle features an open canopy so you can see the world race past. Dramatic and innovative, this racer is low to the ground with its twin-turbo, flat engine and laydown suspension, making it a true concept car!

Born: 2017

SKY FI

Inspired by modern science-fiction movies, the stealthy Sky Fi is on the cutting edge of technology. It features futuristic side jets, a silent tail rotor, and two turbo propellers.

Born: 2019

SKYBOAT

This convertible racer can flip to transform into a helicopter, giving you the ultimate power to out-race your opponents anywhere — by sea or air!

Born: 2019

SLIDE KICK

This hybrid racer pays homage to the original Sidekick from the 1970s. Pull the exhaust pipes and pop open the door to slide the passenger seat out. With its dual-fueling inlets for gasoline and battery charging, and the engine mounted right next to the driver, this modern version of the classic really kicks the competition out of the race!

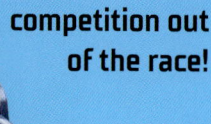

SOLID MUSCLE

Unlike any other pickup, this powerful beast is inspired by drag-racing trucks. Featuring twin nitrous oxide canisters to the rear and active front spoilers, this mean machine has a downforce to be reckoned with and wide rear tires for improved traction.

NETFLIX

The Solid Muscle strong-arms the competition in the animated series.

149

Born: 2020

SPEED DRIVER

This speedster is definitely the right tool for the job. Featuring a wrench and screwdriver, the force of the Speed Driver will have everything spinning in the right direction!

HOT WHEELS FACT

Hot Wheels Let's Race was the #1 TV show for kids on Netflix (US) during its premiere week.

Born: 2017

STREET WIENER

This Street Beast is a feast for the eyes, is a total beast on the track, and is inspired by the designer's love of toy food. It even features a barbeque on the rear of the car that can open and close!

NETFLIX

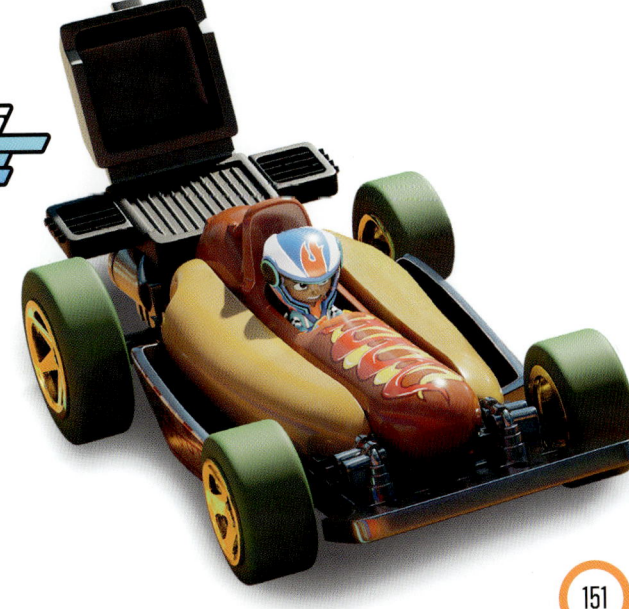

The Street Weiner gets into a sticky situation in the animated series.

Born: 2017

SURF N' TURF

This totally awesome ride is based on the 1950s Woodie. It features a surfboard rack on the roof, a blown big-block engine with side pipes, and a sunroof to catch those rays. Ride the waves with this wagon that's Tooned to the max, dude!

NETFLIX

The Surf N' Turf is featured in the animated series.

SURF DUTY

This rescue vehicle is the premier lifeguard surf patrol machine. Carrying essential equipment, the Surf Duty watches the bay all day and night to save lives—and catch a gnarly tan!

SWEET DRIVER

This dessert ride has everything a great cupcake should have, from the buttercream frosting to the sprinkles on top. Feed your need for speed on the track to sweet, sweet victory!

TEAM HOT WHEELS BUGGY

Born: 2013

This is the die-cast version of the real-wheel-drive performance buggy that completed a record-breaking corkscrew jump. While this car looks like it's made for the dunes, it's probably spent more time in the air.

HOT WHEELS FACT

Two billion wheels are produced per year for Hot Wheels toys.

HOT WHEELS
IN REAL LIFE

This aerodynamic buggy has a 220-horsepower racing engine and a top speed of 120 miles per hour.

A time-lapse photo of the record-breaking jump at the Hot Wheels test facility

THE EMBOSSER

This dependable heavy hauler is designed to leave its mark wherever it goes! Press down on the ramp bed and pack a punch to emboss the Hot Wheels logo on a piece of paper.

Born: 2021

THE NASH

The 2019 Hot Wheels Legends Tour winner rose above thousands of impressive competitors by best representing the true garage spirit of teamwork, innovation, and creativity. Its real-life version went on to win the grand prize at SEMA (Specialty Equipment Market Association)!

Born: 2020

THOMAS & FRIENDS LOCO MOTORIN'

A collaborative design with Thomas & Friends, this train-themed vehicle will run the competition off the rails and onto the track. This wacky racer can do a lot more than pull its weight in a contest!

Thomas the Tank Engine toys have been inspiring imaginations for decades—so it's no wonder the Hot Wheels designers have made a *toot-ally* awesome die-cast model.

Born: 2021

TOONED TWIN MILL

This iconic Hot Wheels vehicle gets a "toon-up" with this hilarious redesign! Stubby and amusingly tall with super-exaggerated twin engines sticking out of the hood, this version brings the car to life with cartoony proportions!

Born: 2020

TOTAL DISPOSAL

The streets of Hot Wheels City will be trash-free with this garbage hauler. It's so stinking cool, no one will be holding their nose when this road rogue rolls up!

Born: 2017

TRACK HAMMER

This two-seater is super lightweight and has a nifty front spoiler that flips up to ace those loops. A roadster with a rear-mounted turbo engine, it can go from zero to sixty in 2.1 seconds. This hammer was built to smash its way around the track!

Born: 2018

TRACK MANGA

This anime-style, gassed-up racer is designed to hit the track for ultimate speed and drift stunts. Featuring twin exhaust pipes and a twin-turbo, four-banger engine, the Track Manga cranks out immense power and superb performance!

Born: 2018

TRACK RIPPER

Built for endurance, this powerful beast of a car is a redefined take on the American muscle car. With its 1,200-horsepower, immense sixteen-cylinder engine, big wings, and a splitter in the front that boosts traction, this ripped racer will leave the other opponents standing!

Born: 2019

TRICERA-TRUCK

Taking inspiration from the Triceratops, this prehistoric creation is pure dino-mite. Featuring a ridged roof, twin front radiators, and a mighty engine, this monstrous truck will roam the earth for many years!

Born: 2022

TROUBLE DECKER

Don't mess with this dragged-out, double-decker bus! Kick it into overdrive for nonstop fun without missing a single stop.

Born: 2019

TUR-BONE CHARGED

Inspired by the Bone Shaker, this sinister ride is the next-generation version! Powered by a giant turbine and with a skull grille and skeletal front fenders, this forbidding challenger is sure to send shivers up and down your spine.

Born: 2022

TURBINE SUBLIME

Sleek and stylish, this racer has two engines and multiple intakes. You'll look cool no matter if you are driving in the past, present, or future.

TURBO ROOSTER

Sporting a twin-turbo, flat six-cylinder motor with 689 horsepower, this "egg-powered" rooster is ready to ruffle some feathers! This Street Beast has a stylized comb, aerodynamic wings, and beak-shaped front end—really giving it something to crow about!

Born: 2021

TURTOSHELL

The Turtoshell is based on a real tortoise named Helix Wheels, who was born without the use of his back legs. After being fitted with a small pair of wheels, Helix was faster than any tortoise around. Just like Helix, the Turtoshell is a cut above the rest!

TWIN MILL

This iconic car is recognized as Hot Wheels's first original design. It has a doorless design with a canopy and two big-block engines for ultimate power.

NETFLIX

In *Hot Wheels Let's Race*, the animated series, Dash Wheeler runs the Ultimate Garage, and the Twin Mill is her favorite car.

HOT WHEELS
IN REAL LIFE

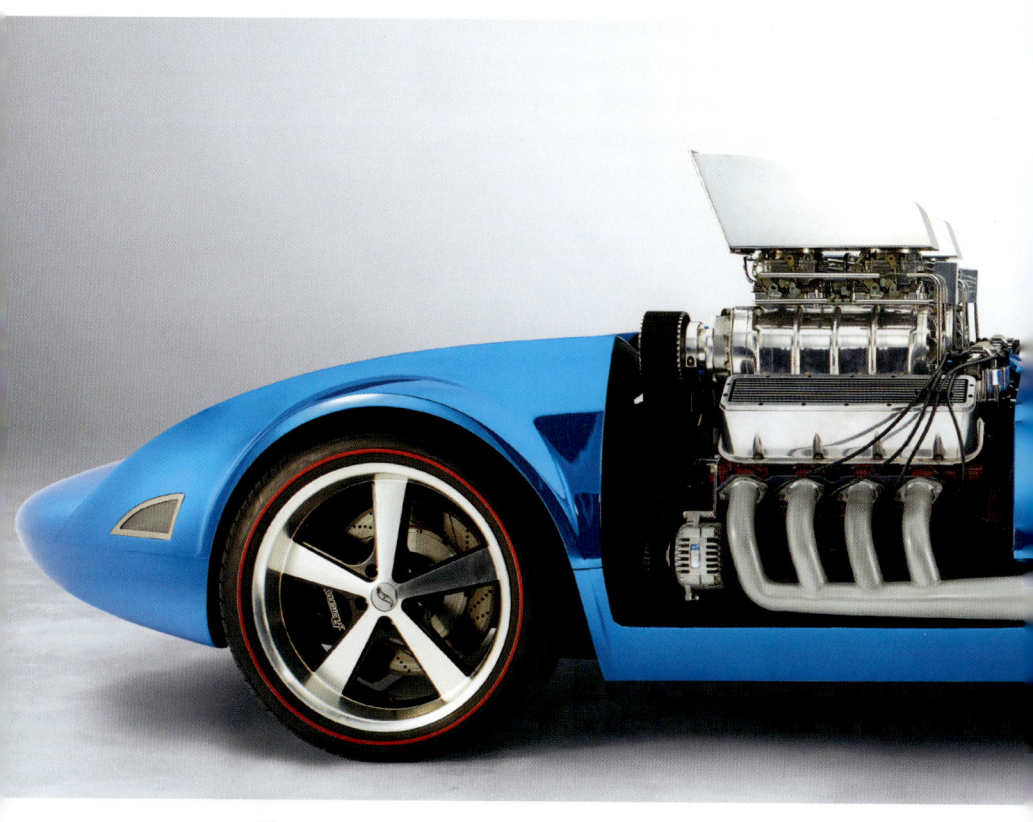

The Twin Mill was the first Hot Wheels full-size car ever built! It features two big-block engines that produce more than 1,400 horsepower. The speedometer jumps from zero to 100 mph in as little as 5.3 seconds—one of the fastest accelerations in the fleet.

TWIN MILL GEN-E

This version of the Hot Wheels favorite is powered by dual high-revving electric motors while maintaining the iconic Twin Mill proportions. With a streamlined driving cockpit and sleek hood, this racer revitalizes this legendary classic.

An original sketch of the Twin Mill

TWINNIN' 'N WINNIN'

It's double the fun, double the adrenaline rush with this off-roader. This two-seater, all-terrain vehicle is designed to chew up and spit out any obstacle that gets in its way!

HOT WHEELS FACT

16.5 Hot Wheels toys are produced per second.

VELOCI-RACER

This prehistoric racer perfectly complements the many dinosaurs on wheels in the world of Hot Wheels. It's a Street Beast that can chase down and capture anything in front of it!

HOT WHEELS FACT

In its first week streaming on Netflix in the US, Hot Wheels Let's Race was watched 16.3 million hours!

Born: 2021

WATER BOMBER

Taking inspiration from classic emergency firefighting aircraft, this rescue vehicle powers up and arrives on the scene to cool things down. The large intakes atop the wings ensure maximum performance and stability, while the force of twin-turbo jets delivers the downpour. With its fully deployed landing gear, the Water Bomber guarantees smooth landings and seamless take-offs!

HOT WHEELS FACT

Hot Wheels has broken three world records: for a distance jump, a corkscrew jump, and a Double Dare Loop stunt.